The Poems of Thomas, Third Lord Fairfax, From Ms. Fairfax 40 in the Bodleian Library, Oxford

TRANSACTIONS OF THE

CONNECTICUT ACADEMY OF ARTS AND SCIENCES

INCORPORATED A. D. 1799

VOLUME 14, PAGES 237-290 JULY, 1909

The Poems of Thomas Third Lord Fairfax

From MS. Fairfax 40

In the Bodleian Library, Oxford

BY

EDWARD BLISS REED

PUBLISHED UNDER THE AUSPICES OF

YALE UNIVERSITY

NEW HAVEN, CONNECTICUT

1909

WEIMAR · PRINTED BY R. WAGNER SOHN

IV.—The Poems of Thomas Third Lord Fairfax

(From the Bodleian MS. Fairfax 40, formerly MS. Add. A. 120.)

In the annals of England the name of Thomas, third Lord Fairfax is deservedly illustrious. As a general he was an intrepid fighter and a skillful commander; in his private life a man of scholarly tastes, happy in his country estates which he preferred to the court. Policy and self-advancement were far from his thoughts despite his great opportunities for aggrandizement; and the simplicity of his character, at which his enemies sneered, was but a proof of his sincerity. To sketch his life in detail is unnecessary, yet his poems will gain significance if, in the briefest manner, we review his interesting career.

The son of Fernandino, second Lord Fairfax, and Mary, daughter of Lord Sheffield, he was born at Denton, Yorkshire, in 1612, of a family long distinguished for its soldierly qualities. In 1620 his grand-father, Thomas, first Lord Fairfax, then a man of sixty, joined with two of his sons, the single regiment sent by James I to the support of the Elector of the Palatinate. He was obliged to return to England to take part in the Parliamentary elections, but his two sons died at Frankenthal at the head of their troops. Fernandino did not make this campaign, and his father spoke of him as a "tolerable country justice, but a mere coward at fighting"[1]; yet Fernandino took the field against Charles I, and certainly did not deserve this taunt.

The early years of our poet were spent in Yorkshire, and he undoubtedly enjoyed in his first studies the guidance of his great uncle, Edward Fairfax, the translator of Tasso. In 1626 he entered St. John's College, Cambridge, where he remained four years, and then, following the family traditions, he went to the Low Countries to serve under Lord Vere against the Spaniards. Another young volunteer in the same camp was Turenne. After witnessing the capture of Bois-le-Duc, he travelled and studied in France for eighteen months, returned to England in 1632, and requested permission to volunteer under Gustavus Adolphus, but his family opposed it, and he retired to the Yorkshire estates to live the life of a country gentle-

[1] *A Life of the Great Lord Fairfax*, by Clements R. Markham. London, 1870, p. 12.

man In 1637 he married the daughter of his commander, Anne Vere a woman of energy and courage, who followed her husband to the field, shared his dangers (she was once taken prisoner by the Royalists) and, in no small measure, determined his career[1]

In the two brief and inglorious Scottish campaigns, Fairfax joined the King's army but when in 1642 Charles came to Yorkshire to seize the supplies at Hull, and raise troops against Parliament the Yorkshire gentry who opposed the King looked to Fairfax for leadership He was entrusted with a formal protest against the King's actions and, despite repulses, succeeded in laying this document on the royal saddle at Heyworth Moor, where Charles was endeavoring to win over the gentry of the shire Fairfax thus showed the world on which side he would be found, and in the Yorkshire campaign that followed, he fought with the greatest courage Undaunted by defeat, fearing no odds, on at least one occasion he attacked a force that outnumbered his own by four to one When surrounded, he cut his way through the enemy At Marston Moor he found himself carried by the tide of battle into the thick of the enemy's ranks Taking from his hat the white badge worn by the Parliamentary forces, he calmly rode through the ranks of the Royalists, regained his troops, and led another attack[2] So fearless was he that on several occasions he narrowly escaped death In 1644 a musket-ball pierced his shoulder, another broke his arm Hardly recovered from these wounds, he was again struck at the siege of Pomfret Castle His skill as a leader, his bravery in action had attracted the attention of all England, and in 1645, when but thirty-three years of age, he was made Commander-in-chief of the Parliamentary forces having as his first task the organization of the New Model army While in the popular opinion it was Cromwell who was "the leading spirit of the war," to quote Sir Clements Markham, the biographer of Fairfax, "it was Fairfax who organized the new army without the smallest assistance from Cromwell It was Fairfax whose genius won the fight at Naseby, and whose consummate generalship concluded the war, and restored peace Cromwell was his very efficient general of horse, but nothing more and indeed he was generally employed on detached duties of secondary importance."[3] At Naseby, Fairfax was conspicuous for his daring; at the surrender of Oxford, he placed a guard about the

[1] *Ibid* p 108
[2] *Ibid*. p 171
[3] *Ibid*, Preface. p iv

Bodleian and saved it from destruction, as he had spared the minster at the siege of York [1]

With Charles hopelessly defeated, Fairfax was unwilling to depose him, wishing the King to rule with the constitution safeguarded from encroachments of the crown He hotly resented the seizure of Charles by Joyce, and through his insistance Charles was allowed to see his friends and above all, his children—a favor for which he repeatedly thanked Fairfax [2] In the political intrigues which preceded the execution of Charles, Fairfax took no part, but when the Royalists made a last stand he laid siege to Colchester, captured the town and crushed the insurrection It was at this time that Milton addressed to him his noble sonnet:

> Fairfax, whose name in arms through Europe rings,
> Filling each mouth with envy or with praise,
> And all her jealous monarchs with amaze,
> And rumours loud that daunt remotest kings,
> Thy firm unshaken virtue ever brings
> Victory home, though new rebellions raise
> Their Hydra heads, and the false North displays
> Her broken league to imp their serpent wings
> O yet a nobler task awaits thy hand
> (For what can war but endless war still breed?)
> Till truth and right from violence be freed,
> And public faith cleared from the shameful brand
> Of public fraud In vain doth Valour bleed
> While Avarice and Rapine share the land

Though appointed one of the Commissioners to try the King, Fairfax refused to be present at the trial and opposed it in vain Surely there are few more dramatic moments in history than when Lady Fairfax rose in the gallery of Westminster Hall to protest against the trial and to defend her husband's name Indeed, so well known was Fairfax's opposition to the execution of the King that Cromwell accused the general of planning to rescue Charles

In 1650 Lord Fairfax resigned his command and returned to his estates at Nunappleton On the death of Cromwell he decided that there would be anarchy unless Charles II returned and ruled Lambert, with a disciplined army of ten thousand men was on the

---

[1] *Ibid* p 271 Fairfax bequeathed to the Bodleian 28 manuscripts See W D Macray *Annals of the Bodleian Library, Oxford*

[2] *Ibid* pp 290 298

field to oppose Monck who, with an army of seven thousand was on the point of declaring for Charles Though ill and suffering intensely, Fairfax sent word to Monck that he would take the field in support of Charles When he appeared, Lambert's troops deserted and flocked to their old commander, and thus, without a shot being fired, the Restoration was accomplished It was fitting that Lord Fairfax should head the commission sent by Parliament to the Hague to invite Charles to return No honors were conferred on him by the Merry Monarch—he sought none—and he retired to Yorkshire, where he died November 12, 1671, three years before the death of Milton

It is not surprising that the letters of Fairfax, and his two *Short Memorials of the War* should have been published, but it is strange indeed that a manuscript of 656 pages of verse, all in his own handwriting, should never have been carefully examined This manuscript passed from the possession of the Fairfax family, and was owned successively by Ralph Thoresby the Duke of Sussex, and Dr Bliss of Oxford from whose collection the Bodleian library, its present owner, purchased it in 1858 Archbishop Cotton in his *Editions of the Bible and Parts thereof in English from the year MDV to MDCCCL*, Preface to the second edition, 1852, gave a table of contents of the manuscript, then in the possession of Dr Bliss, and reprinted one of the paraphrases of the Psalms Sir Clements Markham, in his *Life of Fairfax*, already cited, went further, for in the text of his work he reprinted three of Fairfax's poems,[1] and in an appendix gave ten more, wholly or in part, but as a historian interested in the political, and not the literary life of the times, he made no study of the manuscript Since Markham, I can not find that any one has examined these poems or published them

We have no means of dating the poems with the exception of the following

Upon the New-built House at Apleton (1650), *To the Lady Cary upon her Verses on my deare Wife* (1665), *On the Fatal Day* (1649), *Upon the Horse which his Majestie Rode upon att his Coronation*

[1] *Life of Fairfax* p 352 *On the Fatal Day, Jan 30, 1648*, p 365 *Upon the New-built House at Apleton* p 384 *Upon the Horse which his Majestie Rode upon Att his Coronation* Appendix A, pp 415–427 contains the following *Preface to the Psalms Honny dropps* (excerpts) *The Solitude The Christian Warfare* (excerpts) *Life and Death Compared together Shortness of Life Of Beauty Upon a Patch Face Upon an Ill Husband* and two of the *Vulgar Proverbs*

(1660).[1] As these poems are written down in this order, it will be seen that their position gives no clue to the time of their composition, indeed, the very last poem in the manuscript is an eclogue *Hermes and Lycaon*, by Edward Fairfax who died in 1635.[2] If we refer Fairfax's translations from "good old Mantuan" to his student days, the poems certainly cover a period of forty years.

A perusal of the manuscript shows us at once that Fairfax is not a poet but rather a man of poetic tastes, an admirer of verse. We have, then, no discovery of a neglected genius, and there will be no call for the Complete Works of Thomas Fairfax. It will occasion no surprise, therefore, that we have omitted a considerable amount of his poetry.[3] It will readily be seen that the chief defect in these poems is their poor technique. Fairfax had very little sense of rhythm, at times his ear seems absolutely untrained, and, though a multitude of corrections in the manuscript show how hard he struggled to improve his lines, yet his revisions are generally as awkward as his first rude draft. Few of his poems have any metrical charm, and when in his *Honey Drops* or *Vulgar Proverbs* he seeks to become epigrammatical, he lacks both point and finish. His best writing is seen in such a poem as *David's Lamentation* or in the straightforward couplets of the *Christian Warfare*; however, it is not for his skill as a writer that Fairfax deserves attention but for certain conclusions that may be drawn from the subject-matter of his lines.

Fairfax divided his poetry into religious and secular verse, the former occupying 551 pages out of 650, 388 of these being devoted to a metrical paraphrase of the Psalms. From the days of Wyatt and Surrey in England and Clement Marot in France, to translate the Psalms, or indeed to turn any part of the Scriptures into verse, was a pastime indulged in alike by the devout and by the profligate. A complete list of English writers who from 1500 to 1700 made metrical versions of any portion of the Bible has never been compiled. It would be a surprisingly large one, and though Fairfax was a devout man, he was following a literary fashion as well as his own inclination in his paraphrase, which offers so little that is

[1] The *Epitaph on [illegible] Vere* might be dated were we sure that V stands for Vere.

[2] As Markham published this in *Miscellanies of the Philobiblon Society*, vol. 12, 1868-9, I have not reprinted it.

[3] See table of contents of the MS on page 249. With the exception of the Psalms I have a copy of the whole MS. It is at the disposal of any one interested in it.

interesting that I have reprinted but four Psalms, enough to show his method.[1] In his hymns we notice most of all that he writes in an impersonal style, for we have in them no picture of his own mind, no account of his spiritual conflicts, his doubts, his defeats, or his victories. Religious verse is valuable in proportion as it shows us the soul of a man, and this is precisely what Fairfax does not attempt to do.

This same lack of the personal element in his writing is a marked defect of the secular verse also, for he gives us practically nothing of his own life, even in remote allusion. When we consider the great scenes he had witnessed, the part he had played in shaping the destinies of England, it is rather surprising that he should choose to write on *Envy, Temperance, Anger*. Surely he might have written with more spirit on Liberty, Tyranny, or Valor. He collects many popular proverbs, but he does not jot down the song of his soldiers. For a fighting man, how faint and unrealistic are such lines

> As men besieged with mines about
> Ready to spring and ruing [*sic*] all
> Hearing the alarm beat, runne out
> To th assault and gard ther wall,
> And by the blast in ruins sinke
> Vanquist are when they least thinke.[2]

And yet they are quite unusual, so rarely does he refer to the shock of battle. As Fairfax does not tell us what he has felt, so he has little desire to write down what he has seen. Apart from all considerations of the immeasurable distance that separates Andrew Marvell's work from that of Fairfax, it is yet surprising that Marvell should describe Appleton House and the estates so fully and that Fairfax, who delighted in them, should give us but a few faint lines on the new-built house. Similarly we should expect the sympathetic picture of the last moments of Charles to

---

[1] Markham, in his *Life of Fairfax*, p. 369, mentions another copy of Fairfax's version of the Psalms owned by Mr. Cartwright of Aynho. I have not attempted to trace this. At the end of the MS. of the *Short Memorial*, at Leeds Castle, are versions of the 18th, 24th, 30th and 85th Psalms. He prefaces Psalm 18 with the following: "That I chuse this 18 Psalm let none think that I arrogate anything to myself, for farre be it from me to applie it otherwise than as David's triumph over his enemies." See Markham's *Fairfax*, p. 415.

[2] *A Hymne to Christ the Messiah*.

come from the pen of the general rather than from the tutor of his daughter.[1]

To observe for one's self, to describe one's feelings, demands a certain amount of originality, and this is precisely what Fairfax lacked. The greater part of his religious verse was paraphrase, and we naturally look for translation in his secular poems. Pages 602–10 of the manuscript are taken, he tells us, from the French, the Italian, the Latin. With the exception of the Mazarinades, all these translations are directed against Rome, showing his strong Puritan sympathies. It is interesting to notice that when he translates Petrarch he does not choose the sonnets to Laura, but *The Character of the Romish Church*.[2] Petrarchism, brought in by Wyatt and Surrey a century before, had spent its force, and the lyrics of Philip Ayres, 1687, fill the last book that shows the old sway of the founder of the modern lyric.[3] As confirmation of Fairfax's lack of skill in writing, it is noticeable that he is unable to reproduce the sonnet form, and turns the quatorzains into poems of twelve lines.

Eight pages of translation, however, constitute but a small part of his secular verse. As we read it, we are impressed by the contrasts it shows, contrasts that can not be explained by assuming that certain poems are separated by long intervals of time. Lady Carey had written to Fairfax a metrical epistle on the death of his wife, and he felt called upon to answer it. Knowing his devotion to Lady Fairfax, we expect him to rise above himself under the inspiration of his grief, but his thought is so trivial and so feebly expressed that *To the Lady Cary Upon her Verses on my deare Wife* is one of the poorest poems. A few lines will show this more plainly than any comment.

Madam

> Could I a Tribute of my thanks express
> As you have done in love and purer verse,
> On my best selfe then I might justly raise
> Your Elogy & Encomiums of your Prayse
> And soe forgett the Subject that did move
> Me to a thankfulness as it did you to love
> O twere to great a Crime but pray allow

[1] See Marvell's *Horatian Ode upon Cromwell's Return from Ireland*.
[2] Sonnets *De Laura In morte*, Nos. 11 and 16.
[3] *Lyric Poems, made in Imitation of the Italians*, London, 1687.

> Wher I fall short but you have reached to
> Making that Good wisest of Kings hath said,
> Th Livings not soe Prayse-worthy then [*sic*] the dead

A few pages further on, we come to a more formal elegy on Henry of Navarre

> Ah is itt then Great Henry soe fam'd
> For taming men, himselt by death is tam'd!
> Whatt eye his glory saw, now his sad doome,
> But must desolve in Teares, sigh out his Soule,
> Soe small a shred of Earth should him intombe
> Whos acts deserv'd pocession of the whole

Though this poem has its defects, it is, on the whole, a better piece of writing than the elegy on Lady Fairfax This consideration, together with the fact that Henry of Navarre was assassinated two years before Fairfax was born, and that there seems to be no special reason why he should lament his death, makes one suspect that the lines are a translation from the French Such is the case, for I find that the poem is taken word for word from an elegy by Anne de Rohan which Fairfax read at the end of Agrippa d'Aubigne's *Histoire Universelle*, published 1626, for d'Aubigne does not quote the whole poem and Fairfax translates only as much as he gives [1] With this hint I have looked in the French literature of the period for the originals of the other poems *On a Fountain* is a translation of an epigram of Malherbe that was a favorite one [2] to judge from its appearance in a French anthology (*Les Delices de la Poesie Françaıse* 1615), while Fairfax's best poem the one that gives the manuscript its title, is a translation of Saint-Amant's *La Solitude* Other sources I have not found but I feel convinced that many of the poems are translations, as for example, *Of a Faire Wife, to Coregio* which is probably taken from the Italian Others better read in Continental literature of the period may discover his models [3]

We are now in a position to see the significance of these poems They are not fine examples of English verse, they are rather to be regarded as documents that show us what an English gentleman

[1] *Histoire Universelle* par Agrippa d'Aubigne (Paris, 1879) Vol 9, pp 172–75

[2] See *Oeuvres complètes* de Malherbe (Paris, 1862), Vol 1, p 225

[3] Mr Lewis C Everard Yale Phi Beta Kappa Fellow 1908–1909, has searched in the Bibliotheque Nationale, Paris, for other French originals, but without results

of the Caroline and Commonwealth period read and thought. They are like an old diary in which a great man has jotted down a list of the books he owns, or of poems he has memorized; they are like a package of old letters, in which the writer tells us of his favorite authors and his literary tastes. It is to be observed that this moralist who mentions but one English writer—his great-uncle—turns to French literature. *La Solitude* is certainly not only Saint-Amant's best piece of work but one of the finest French poems of the period, and the evident admiration of Fairfax for it speaks well for his taste. Though Saint-Amant had twice visited London and was possibly known there as a poet, only two other unimportant translations of his verse have been noticed in English literature.[1] It is worthy of mention that Saint-Amant himself had some very pronounced opinions concerning Fairfax, who probably never read the Frenchman's *Epigramme Endiablée sur Fairfax*.[2]

There is another interesting point concerning *La Solitude*. It is well known that in 1650 Andrew Marvell came to Appleton House as a tutor for Mary Fairfax. He had already written verse, but it had not been nature-poetry; his grotesque *Flecnoe* and his absurd verses *Upon the Death of Lord Hastings* have nothing of the meadow

[1] See A. H. Upham, *The French Influence in English Literature from the Accession of Elizabeth to the Restoration*, New York, 1908, pp. 315, 405, 409–412. It is interesting to read Saint-Amant's brief reference to Ben Jonson in his *L'Albion*.

[2] Je crois qu'il doit bien estre en peine
L'execrable tyran qui preside aux enfers,
Quand, dans les feux et dans les fers,
Il songe au noir object des foudres de ma haine.
Son vieux sceptre enfumé tremble en sa fiere main;
Il redoute Fairfax, ce prodige inhumain;
Il craint que ce monstre n'aspire
Au degré le plus haut de son horrible empire.
Le degré le plus haut est celuy le plus bas;
C'est *où ce prince des sabats*,
Des endroits les plus clairs aux endroits les plus sombres,
Tomba pour regner sur les ombres.
C'est là, dis-je, qu'il craint que par quelque attentat,
Que par quelque moyen oblique,
Fairfax n'aille du moins renverser son estat
Pour en faire une republique.
Et voilà les raisons qui l'ont fait hesiter
Jusqu'à cette heure à l'emporter.

Œuvres Complètes de Saint-Amant (Paris, 1855), vol. I, p. 472.

in them During the two years he spent at the home of Fairfax Marvell wrote those nature-poems that determined his fame—*Upon the Hill and Grove at Billborow*, *Upon Appleton House*, *On a Drop of Dew*, *The Garden*—poems that show an observation an apprecation of the earth, of flowers, birds and trees unsurpassed in all the works of his predecessors in English poetry, not excepting the very greatest, Chaucer Spenser, and Shakespeare That these poems were inspired not only by the beauty of Nunappleton, but by its owners love and appreciation of poetry, there can be little doubt We may go even further, and see in Marvell's nature-poems some hints from Saint Amant Marvell's verse is richer and deeper, where Saint-Amant is vague in his descriptions or conventional in his thought, Marvell is concrete and original, for it is the Englishman, and not the Frenchman, who uses *le mot precis*, and yet Saint-Amant's theme—to lose one's self in Nature—is the theme of *The Garden* and of the finest lines in *Appleton House*

We see now the significance of the poems of Fairfax They throw light on the character of a great Englishman; they remind us that the literary influence of *la ville lumiere* was still powerful in England, that it had not died with the sonneteers, and they give us the atmosphere in which Andrew Marvell lived and wrote the tenderest, the sincerest, the deepest nature-poetry of the seventeenth century

Yale College,
February 19, 1909

EDWARD BLISS REED

TABLE OF CONTENTS OF MS. FAIRFAX 16

The poems marked † are reprinted here. Those marked are given only in part. The poems are printed as they stand in the MS. with no changes in the punctuation or spelling.

[Title] THE IMPLOYMENT OF MY SOLITUDE T. F. p. i

† The Preface to the Psalmes p. ii

Psalms 1 to 150, in verse pp. 1–388 [p. 389 is blank.]

Songs of the Old and New Testament pp. 390–479

Moses Songe Exodus 15 p. 390

Moses Songe Deut. 32 p. 396

The Songe of Deborah Judges 5 p. 406

Hannah's Songe 1 Sam. 2 p. 415

† Dauids Lamentation for Saule & Jonathan 2 Sam. 1 p. 418

† Hezekiah's Songe Isaiah 38 p. 422

The Songe of Mary the Blessed Virgin Luke 1 p. 427

Zachariah's Songe Luke 1 p. 429

† Simeon's Songe p. 431

† The Songe of Salomon Chapter 1 p. 432 Chapt. 2 p. 435
Chapt. 3 p. 438 Chapt. 4 p. 440 Chapt. 5 p. 444
Chapt. 6 p. 448 Chapt. 7 p. 451 Chapt. 8 p. 454

Out of the Prouerbs of Salomon p. 458

Wisdom's Antiquity pp. 471-475

Out of the Prouerbs of Salomon p. 473[b] 473[c]

[These two pages were formerly pasted together. They are a repetition of pp. 458 and 459, with two lines of 460.]

Samuel's Instruction from his Mother Prouerbs 32 p. 476

† Honny dropps p. 480

Hymnes to the Soueraine God p. 510

A Hymne to Christ the Mesiah p. 519

A Hymne to the Holy Ghost p. 539

† A Songe of Prayse p. 549–551[a]

[Title] The Recreations of my Solitude T. F. p. 551[c]

† The Solitude p. 552

† Of a Faire Wife to Coregio p. 564

† Of Beauty p. 568

† Upon a Patch Face p. 570

Upon a Younge Virago p. 571

† Upon an ill Husband p. 571

† Of Envy p. 572

† Of Anger p. 574

† Of Virtue p. 577

Of Patience and Temperance p. 579

† Nature and Fortune p 582
† The Christian Warfare p 583
† Life and Death compared together p 590
† Upon a Fountaine p 592
† Upon the New-built House at Apleton p 593
† Shortness of Life p 594
† Epitaph on A V dieng Younge p 595
† The Lady Caryes Elogy on my deare Wife p 596
† To the Lady Cary Upon her Verses on my deare Wife p 598
† On the Fatal Day, Jan 30th, 1648 p 600
† Of Impartial Fate p 601
Epitaph sur le Mort du Cardinal Mazarin Epiodium p 602
† A Carracter of the Romish Church by Francisco Petrarca, Laura Can 106 p 604
Pontanus writes this Epitaph on Lucretia daughter of Alexander 6 p 606
Baptista Mantua reproving the wicked Life of Sixtus 4 maketh the Divel give him this Entertainement in Hell p 607
Mantua Eclogae 5 p 608
Palengenus A Papist thus discribes the monstrous Corruptions of the Romaine Clargie p 609
Upon Mr Stanley's Booke of Philosophers supposing itt the Worke of his Tutor W. Fa p 611
† Upon the Horse wch his Matie Rode upon att his Coronation 1660 p 612
Vulgar Proverbs p 613
† The teares of France for the deplorable death of Henry 4 surnamed the Great p 641
An Egloge made by my uncle Mr Ed Fairfax in a Dialoge betwixt two Sheapards Hermes and Lycaon p 647

[p ii]

The Preface to the Psalmes

Vaine Fancy whether now darst thou aspire
W^th smoky Coales to light the holy Fire
Could thou indeed as wth the Phenix burne
In perfum'd flames & into Ashes turne
Thou might'st hope (vaine hope) yet once againe
To rise wth purer notions in thy Braine
But t'would nott serue for they would still be darke
Till from thyn Alter Lord I take a sparke
I need not then assend up any higher
In offring this to fetch another fire
Inspired thus may on my Muse distill
Dewes nott from Parnass but Hermans sweet Hill

[p 1]

Psal 1

Blest is the man in walking daly shuns
Pernitious Councel that from th' wicked Comes
Nor to the sinners paths his steps doth bend
Or he yitt up to Scorners chaire assend
Who in the early morne & euening laite
On lawes deuine makes choyse to meditate
As by the runing streames the well sett tree
His fruit in season yeild, the iust shall be
Whos leafe shall neuer fade & what he doth
Shall thriue as itt & shal be fruitfull both
But wth the wicked itt is diffrent faire
As chaff tost in the Ayre, So they are
Nor shall he stand fore th' impartial Judge
Or mongst the iust who in sins way doe trudge

[p 38]

Psal 19

The heauens Lord the siluer studed frame
They are the Curious works thy hands declare
Time vnto time itt doth recount the same
To places most remote, ther voyce it heares
Ore all the earth ther arched Sphers extends
The Tun on's throne ther rises ther desends

As cherfull brid-grome in his nuptial state
Or actiue men to race wth ioy Come out
From East to West so runs he at that raute
Till his cirquitt rownd he'as gone about
All parts euen to the wide Earths extreames
Both light & heat takes from his radent beames

[p 39] Thy law ô Lord to soules perfection giues
They that are simple by thy words made wise
They shall reioyce who in thy precepts liues
Thy Statutes pure inlightens the blind eyes
To feare the Lord will vs preserue for euer
Whos iudgments true & rightious altogether

More sweete then honny yea or gold refin d
Thy seruants setts them att a hier prise
They great rewards in keeping them do find
But o alas who ist his errors spies
My faults vnseene ô let ther none remaine
From bold-fac d sins thy seruant Lord restraĩe

[p 40] O let not sin wth it's tyranick might
Ere gitt a iuri[s]diction ouer mee
So in my soule shall I then be vpright
And from the great transgression guiltless be
So shall my words & thoughts acceptance find
Wth thee my strength redeemer of man-kind

[p 49] Psal 23

How can I want the Lord my sheapard seemes
Who to the verdant pasturs leads me outt
By flowry bankes wher waters gently streams
My soule he doth refresh he sets my foot
In paths of truth & eaqual Justice both
This only for his owne name sake he doth

Al though I through death[s] shady vale doe goe
No terrors ther shal makes me yitt affraid
His rods my guide his staff my strength also
Before myn foes my table he doth spread
Wth oyle my head full cups my hart doth chere
Him in his house for euer I le serue ther

[p. 104] Psal 46

If in distresse Lord thou 'lt giue me ayde
What need I feare though rocks in seas be throwe
Though by ther rage the hills on hills be layd
Thou still preseruest thos that are thyn owne
In thes ore turnings shal noe fear cease them
For God was ther, his help in season Came

When furious rage procest the Heathen world
Thou was to vs as a strong Towre in War
Thou spake the word & Earth on heaps was hurld
Come se then ther what great vastations are

[p. 105] T'is he when wars arise Can stop ther Course
This he ther weapons breake ther Chariots fire
Wait thou on him know he's a God of force
Did he not rule the world t' would soone expire
He mongst the Heathens will exalted be
But Jacobs Gods the Towre to whom we flee

[p. 390] Songs of the Old & New
Testment

Moses Songe
Exodus 15

Vnto the Lord let prayse be sung
 Who gloriously triumphed hath
For he into the sea hath flung
 Both Horse & Rider in his wrath

The Lord my strength & songe shall be
 Who my sure saluation
Mine & my father's god is he
 Soule be his habitation

[p. 391] A man of Warr's the Lord renown'd
 His name is by Jehouah knowne
Who in the Sea hath Pharoah drownd
 Downe Captains Horse & Chariots throwne

This goodly Traine wth fury drunke
 The waues as Coueringes did Containe

Wher to the bottome they are sunke
   As stones that neuer rise againe

Thy hand o Lord has done this deed
   Glorious in Powre art thou become
Thy hand I say when ther was need
   Th insulting Foe has ouercome

[p 392] They that agaist thee did Combine
   Thy wrath has broke in thy defence
As stuble th are before the winde
   So powrefull is thyn excelence

Thy Nosthrills wth a blast haue layde
   The liquid Seas on sollid heapes
The floating waues ther wth were stay d
   As Ice Congealed in the depths

Pursue oretake th' enmy said
   Ther spoyles let vs mongst vs deuide
Whilst wth ther Swords they hauack made
   And lust as law to them was guide

[p 393] But in a happy howre thou did
   The Treasures of thy winde display
So sunk they as the heauy lead
   And vnder watry-Mountains lay

Amongst the Gods whos like to thee
   O Lord in Holiness & Prayse
The fearfull wonders wch we see
   Doe Trophyes to thy Glory raise

Thou stretcht thy hand & they were gone
   The gapinge earth deuourd them quite
To th Holy mountaine thou leddst on
   The chosen Flock of thy delight

[p 394] Nations hard this wth pale-faced looks
   And horred feare amazed stood
Edom Moab & Syrian Dukes
   Ditt melt away wt Canans broode

Thy Glorious Name did soe apall
   Ther trembling Harts wth feare & dread
That as a stone lie still they shall
   Till those pass ouer thou dost lead

To Zions mount thou didst them bring
Didst plant them in its fertil soyle
The place wher thou delightst in
A sanctuary freed from toyle

[p 395] Raigne Lord for euer vn-opposd
For Pharoa's Horse & Men are drownd
Him & his force hath sea inclosd
Whilst Israel marches on dry grownd

Miriam the Prophetiss a Timbrel takes
Wher in their Circulinge-dances round
The Virgin-Traine such Musick makes
As th Hills about wth Ecchoes sound

Then Miriam answered them & sunge
The Lord triumphd in Glory hath
Proud Pharoah into th' sea has flunge
Wth Horse & Rider in his wrath

[p 418] Dauids Lamentation for Saule & Jonathan

2 Sam 1

Israel has lost her ornement
Alas for itt lement
How are her Mighty, falne & lame
& on Mount Gibea slaine
Ô let itt nott in Gath be knowne
Or told in streets of Askelon

O lett nott Lord our ancient Foes
Joying Deride our woes
Least daughter of th' vncircomcis'd
Triumph o're vs dispis'd
[p 419] Noe more lett fruitfull showres distill
Or dewes on Gibeas direfull Hill

Nor e'er may any thither bringe
More a Heaue-Offringe
Ther th' Mighty fell, Saule lost his sheild
In this shamfull feild
On him regardless they did treade
As if noe oyle had touch'd his head

Sharp Arrowes shott from Jonathans Bow
Drunk wth the blood of Foe
Nor did Sauls sword rebate a Jott
Till he'ad his[1] enmys smote
[p 120] How louely-pleasant are you tow
Death Could not loue disjoyne in you

Swifter then Eagles wch th' Ayre peirce
Both stronge as lions feirce
Israel's daughters lement the fall
Of your valiant Saule
Who you in Purple & Scarlet deckt
And did from Foes your land protect

How pleasant was itt to behold
Your ornments of Gold
Thy worthys by the sword how are
They thus cutt off in war

[p 121] O Jonathan my harts delight
Slaine in the bloody fight
Mount Giboa saw the woefull day
Thou mongst her Rockes ther wounded lay

How can I Deare Jonathan express
For thee my sad distress
Noe Woman's loue reach'd thatt degree
As thou once loued mee
How is the Mighty falne, is Crusht
And Israels Worthys rould in dust

[p 122] Hezekiahs-Songe

Isaiah 38

In Cuttinge off my days I said
Must I goe downe to deaths cold shade
Youth's flowre noe sooner Budd but Blast
Be Cropt and to oblivion cast
Mongst living Lord must I noe more
Lift vp myn eyes & thee adore

[1] Fairfax has written over this line 'his foes had smote'

Or longer in this vniuerse
W^th Man-kind haue noe more Conuerse
Farwell then Suns chearful light
Whose Rayes expells the shades of Night
[p. 423] Adeiu deare siluer-Horned Moone
By step & step our time setts downe
Yee Stars farwel that in Night appears
Runing in your apoynted Spheres
Who from your orbs soe far from hence
Throwes downe on vs your influence
Stay when you will your Constant Course
For ouer death you haue noe force
Farwel my Friends, farwel delight
Deuided by Eternal Night
My flitting years how soon th are spent
Remoued as a Sythian Tent
Here to day to morrow dead
[p. 424] Cut off like to a weauers thread
In morning when new hopes began
Er euening pining sickness came
Yitt didst nott heare my sad groanes
But lyon-like brake all my bones
O whatt a little space is this
Twixt Being & not Beinge is
Euen from th Eueninge to the Day
My wasting Sperits fade away
As Crane or Swallow sett alone
To the ô Lord I make my mo'ne
And as the Doue that trembling sitts
When Hawke aboue doth sores his pitch
[p. 425] So faints my hart so failes myn eyes
In seing such sad miseryes
But thou in Mercy hast noe piere
O help me in this troubled feare
What shall I say but sure thus much
Thy Word & Truth keep perfait touch
For sin my soule shall all itts days
Walke softly in my pensiue wayes
By these things Lord doe Mortals liue
New life by these things thou dost giue
Lo, Peace to me dost thou restore
And Joy for Greefe I had before

Thou pluckt me from destrictions Pitt
[p 426] And all my sins didst thou remitt
For who in death can offrings bringe
Or in the Graue thy Prayses singe
Or All to Shades beneath repare
Does any hope for Mercy ther
The liuinge tis the liuinge They
Shall Prayse thee as I doe this day
Father to sonne relate shall this
How faithfull are thy Promises
Since Lord thou hast prolong'd my days
On Warbling Harpe Ile giue thee prayse
And in thy Courts wth Holy Fire
Of Zeale pay thanks till I expire

[p 431] Simeons Songe

As thou hast said soe Lord pray I
In peace now lett thy seruant die
Sence my blest eyes haue seene ith end
Saluation from thy Throne desend
Which thou before earth frame was layd
To saue Man-kind decreed had
A light to guide the Gentiles ways
Of Israels sones to be the prayse

[p 435] [The Songe of Salomon]

Chap 2

I am the Rose of Sharons fruitfull feild
The Lilly wch the humble vallyes yeild
In midst of thornes as Lilly appears aboue
Soe mongst the youthfull Virgins is my loue
As Apple-trees mongst trees oth Forrest growe
Amongst the sones of Men my loue is soe
Vnder whose shade is my delightfull seat
And to my tast his fruit is pleasant meat
Then to the house of wines he brought me in
Wher Loue like banners was a Couer in
Stay me wth flaggons wth Apples Comfort giue
Who's sick of Loue may yitt haue hope to liue

Vnder my head his left hand stretched out
And wth his Right h' imbraceth me about
[p 436] O Zions daughters I strictly you admire
By the swift Hynde & fearfull Roe be sure
Noe stir by noyse you make for to disease
Or wake my loue before the time he please
Behold I hear his Voyce o're Hills & Downes
My loue Comes skiping ouer Mounts & bounds
Like th Hart or nimble Fawne & triping Roe
Standing behind our Wall Behold him Loe
Through trelest windows how he looketh out
His Church wth watchfull care he vews about
Thus speaking to me I my loue did heare
Arise my faire one Come away my deare
Lo winters past wth her stormy showers
Th' Earth now shew's her various coulred flowrs
Chirping of birds a signe the spring grows near
[p 437] We in the land the mourning Turtle heare
The Figg-tree budding green her Figgs disclose
The tender Grapes of Vines smell as the Rose
Arise my faire one Come away my loue
Whom Clifty Rocks doe hid Come out my Doue
Shew me thy Face myn eares let thy Voyce meet
Thy Countinance is Comely, Voyce most Sweet
Take th' Fox & little Foxes in thy Toyles
That thus our tender grapes & Vinyard spoyles
My deare is myne & I am his who 'monge
The Lillyes feed till shades of Night be gone
Turne my beloued turne like th Roe that trips
Or nimble Hinde that in Mount Bether skips

[p 480] Honny dropps

(Under this title Fairfax has written
one hundred and twenty five couplets and thirty five quatrains)

Why good men haite all sin tis understood
Because tis both gainst god and ther owne good

To walke wth god tis goodmen s care we see
But leaves the Care to god wch way 't should be

Noe safty wth out god in Freindship were
Yitt safe wth enimyes if God be there

[p 482] A good man questionless was never hee
Thatt strives nott allways better for to be

[p 483] Good Conscience is a name att wch Men taunt
But betters a good name then Conscience want

[p 484] Whatt before men we are affrayd to doe
Fore God to thinke itt should affright us too

Many the Sacred ordinances use
Making noe proffet of them—them abuse

[p 186] When thou dost well or any good thou can
Prayse nott thy worke, the worke will prayse the Man

[p 487] The soule by such a Noble spirit moves
Tis nott soe much where t lives as wher it loves

Sure best are they, nott they who most can talke
How Good God is, but who most with him walke

[p 490] In sweetest Natures this will sure befall
None All can like nor shall be likt of all

[p 491] All Earthly things are such as ther s noe doubt
Worst Men may have and best may goe w^th^outt
Yett wanting them a man may happy be
When others wth them have butt misery

[p 492] Noe Time in pastime need we Idly wast
For time will pass from us in too much hast

[p 507] I'th' Sacred Arke Reason of State should lye
But rules of state should nott Religion tye

When men wth wine themselves like beasts abuse
Not wine the Men but the wine misuse

[p 509] In all thou undertakes be carful still
That none of thee can spe the deserved ill
And soe when that is done thou needs not Care
For Ill mens Censure (Tis the Common fate)

[p 549] A Songe of Prayse

Earth prayse the Lord him Reverence beare
As well for's Thunders that we heare
At wch poore Mortals stand affraid

As four the glorious Maruels which
Such Splendors doth the world inrich
They are the workes his hands hath made

His Prouidential loue lets singe
That wth a plentious flowinge springe
Our barren soules hee watered

The East the West tast of his Care
Hott Affrick nor the freezinge Beare
From his al seeinge eye is hidd

[p 550] And wast nott he He who did please
Wth seueral kinds to store the Seas
Of Fish beyond account Nay more

Made Woods & Hills that Cataile yeilds
Gaue flowry Pasturs verdent feilds
That bringe both Corne & wine great store

But how doe we his mercy wronge
He sees wee still in Sin grow stronge
And day by day his patience moue

Yet as a Father ready is
To pardon faults he sees in his
Such are the tokens of his loue

[p 551 a] In vs Affections ôh tis strange
Wth our light humor suddaine Change
As in a moment they grew old

They wth the Wind are easely driuen
But his is alweyes firme & euen
And to Eternity doe hold

Finis

[p 551 e] The Recreations of my Solitude

T F

[p 552] THE SOLITUDE

O how I loue these Solitudes
And places silent as the Night
Ther wher noe thronging multituds
Disturbe wth noyse ther sweet delight
O how myn eyes are pleas'd to see
Oakes that such spreadinge branches beare
Wch from old Times nativity
And th'envy of so many yeares
Are still greene beautifull & faire
As att the world's first day they were

Naught but the highest twiggs of all
Wher Zephyrus doth wanton play
[p 553] Doe yett presage ther future fall
Or shew a signe of ther decay
Times past Fawnes Satyrs Demy-Gods
Hither retir'd to seeke for Aide
When Heauen wth Earth was soe att odds
As Jupiter in rage had laide
Ore all a Deluge these high woods
Preseru'd them from the sweling floods

Ther vnder a flowry Thorne alonge
Of Springs delightfull plant the Cheife
Sadd Philomela's mournfull songe
Doth sweetly entertaine my greefe
And to behold is noe less rare
[p 554] These hanging Rocks & Precepices
Wch to the wounds of sadd dispare
Are soe propitious to giue ease
When soe oprest by cruel fate
Death's sought for att another gate

[LA SOLITUDE][1]

A Alcidon

Que j'ayme la solitude!
Que ces lieux sacrez à la nuit,
Esloignez du monde et du bruit,
Plaisent à mon inquietude!
Mon Dieu! que mes yeux sont contens
De voir ces bois, qui se trouverent
A la nativité du temps,
Et que tous les siecles reverent,
Estre encore aussi beaux et vers,
Qu'aux premiers jours de l'univers!

Un gay zephire les caresse
D'un mouvement doux et flatteur.
Rien que leur extresme hauteur
Ne fait remarquer leur vieillesse.
Jadis Pan et ses demy-dieux
Y vindrent chercher du refuge,
Quand Jupiter ouvrit les cieux
Pour nous envoyer le deluge,
Et, se sauvans sur leurs rameaux,
A peine virent-ils les eaux.

Que sur cette espine fleurie,
Dont le printemps est amoureux,
Philomele, au chant langoureux,
Entretient bien ma resverie!
Que je prens de plaisir à voir
Ces monts pendans en precipices,
Qui, pour les coups du desespoir,
Sont aux malheureux si propices,
Quand la cruauté de leur sort
Les force a rechercher la mort!

[1] This is not in the MS. See pp. 246–248.

How pleasant are the Murmuring stream
In shady Vallyes runinge downe
Whose raginge torrents as itt seemes
Just measurs keepe in skipps & bounds
Then glidinge vnder th arbored banks
As windinge Serpents in the grass
The sportfull Naides playes ther pranks
[p 555] Vpon the watry plaines of Glass
The christal Elements wherin
These watry Nimphes delight to swime

The quiet Marshe I loue to see
That bounded is wth willowes round
With Sallow Elme, & Popler tree
Wch Iron yett hath giuen noe wound
The Nimphes that Come to take fresh Ayre
Here Rocks & Spindles them prouide
Mongst Sedge & Bulrush we may heare
The lepinge Froggs Se wher they hide
Themselues for feare when they espye
A Man or Beast approachinge nye

[p 556] A hundred thousand Fowle her lye
All voyd of feare makinge ther Nest
Noe treachrous Fowler here Comes nye
Wth mortal gunnes to breake ther rest
Some toying in the sunns warme beames
Ther fethers busily doe plume
Whilst others findinge Loues hott flames
In waters allsoe can Consume
And in all pastimes Inocent
Are pleased in this Element

How pleasant is itt to behold
These ancient Ruinated Towers
[p 557] 'Gainst wch the Giants did of old
Wth Insolence imploye ther Powers
Now Sayters here ther Sabath keepe
And Sperits wch our sence inspire
Wth frightinge dreames whilst we doe sleepe
Noe here againe all day retire
In thousand Chinkes & dusty holes
Lyes vgly Batts & Scritchinge Owles

Que je trouve doux le ravage
De ces fiers torrens vagabonds,
Qui se precipitent par bonds
Dans ce valon vert et sauvage!
Puis, glissant sous les arbrisseaux,
Ainsi que des serpens sur l'herbe,
Se changent en plaisans ruisseaux,
Ou quelque Naiade superbe
Regne comme en son lict natal,
Dessus un throsne de christal!

Que j'aime ce marets paisible!
Il est tout borde d'aliziers,
D'aulnes, de saules et d'oziers,
A qui le fer n'est point nuisible.
Les Nymphes, y cherchans le frais,
S'y viennent fournir de quenouilles,
De pipeaux, de joncs et de glais;
Où l'on voit sauter les grenouilles,
Qui de frayeur s'y vont cacher
Si tost qu'on veut s'en approcher.

La, cent mille oyseaux aquatiques
Vivent, sans craindre, en leur repos,
Le giboyeur fin et dispos,
Avec ses mortelles pratiques.
L'un, tout joyeux d'un si beau jour,
S'amuse a becqueter sa plume;
L'autre allentit le feu d'amour
Qui dans l'eau mesme se consume,
Et prennent tous innocemment
Leur plaisir en cet element.[1]

Que j'ayme a voir la decadence
De ces vieux chasteaux ruinez,
Contre qui les ans mutinez
Ont deploye leur insolence!
Les sorciers y font leur sabat;
Les demons follets s'y retirent,
Qui d'un malicieux ebat
Trompent nos sens et nous martirent;
La se nichent en mille troux
Les couleuvres et les hyboux.

[1] Fairfax omits a stanza here.

These Mortal Augurs of Mischance
Who funerall notes as Musick makes
The Goblins singe & skipp & dance
In valts ore spred wth Toads & Snakes
Ther in a Cursed beame might see
[p 558] The horred Skelton of some poore louer
W^{ch} for his Mistriss Cruelty
Hanged himselfe sence naught could moue her
Or wth a glance nott once to daine
To ease him of his mortal paine

The Marble Stones here strew'd about
Of Caracters leaue yett some signe
But now are almost eaten outt
By teeth of all deuouring time
The planks & timber from aboue
Downe to the lowest Valts are fau'ne
Wher Toads & Vipers 'mongst them moue
Leauinge theron ther deadly spawne
[p 559] And Harths that once were vs'd fyr fyers
Now shaded are wth scratchinge Bryers

Yet lower an Arched-Valt extends
Soe hiddious darke & deepe doth sinke
That did the Sun therin desend
I thinke he scarce Could se a winke
Slumber that from heauy Cares
Wth drowsiness inchants our sence
Sleepes here secure as far from feares
Lul'd in the Armes of Negligence
And on her back in sluggish sort
Vpon the pauement lyes & Snort

[p 560] When from these Ruings I doe goe
Vp an aspiringe Rock nott farre
Whose topp did seeme as't were to know
Wher mists & Stormes ingendred are
And then desending att my leasure
Downe paths made by the storming Waues
I did behold wth greater pleasure
How they did worke the hollow Caues
A worke soe Curious & soe rare
As if that Neptuns Court were ther

L'orfraye, avec ses cris funebres,
Mortels augures des destins,
Fait rire et dancer les lutins
Dans ces lieux remplis de tenebres
Sous un chevron de bois maudit
Y branle le squelette horrible
D'un pauvre amant qui se pendit
Pour une bergere insensible,
Qui d'un seul regard de pitie
Ne daigna voir son amitie. [1]

La se trouvent sur quelques marbres
Des devises du temps passe,
Icy l'age a presque efface
Des chiffres taillez sur les arbres,
Le plancher du lieu le plus haut
Est tombe jusques dans la cave,
Que la limace et le crapaut
Souillent de venin et de bave,
Le lierre y croist au foyer,
A l'ombrage d'un grand noyer

La dessous s'estend une voûte
Si sombre en un certain endroit,
Que quand Phebus y descendroit,
Je pense qu'il n'y verroit goutte,
Le Sommeil aux pesans sourcis,
Enchante d'un morne silence,
Y dort, bien loing de tous soucis,
Dans les bras de la Nonchalence,
Laschement couche sur le dos
Dessus des gerbes de pavos [1]

Tantost, sortant de ces ruines,
Je monte au haut de ce rocher,
Dont le sommet semble chercher
En quel lieu se font les brunes,
Puis je descends tout a loisir,
Sous une falaise escarpee,
D'ou je regarde avec plaisir
L'onde qui l'a presque sappee
Jusqu'au siege de Palemon,
Fait d'esponges et de limon

---

[1] Fairfax omits a stanza here

Tis a delightfull sight to see
Standinge on the murmuringe shore
[p 561] When Calmer Seas begin to bee
After the Stormes wth raginge roare
How the blew Trytons doe appeare
Vpon the rollinge Curled Waues
Beatinge wth hiddious tunes the Ayre
W^th^ Crooked Trumpets Sea-men braues
Att whose shrill notes the winds doe seeme
By keepinge still to beare esteeme

Sometimes the Sea wth Tempests tore
Frettinge itt Can rise noe higher
Roulinge or'e the flinty shore
Throwes them vp againe retires
[p 562] Somtimes through itt's deuouringe Jawes
When Neptun's in an angry moode
Poore mariners finde his Cruel lawes
Made to his tiny Subiects foode
But Diamonds Amber & the Jett
To Neptune they doe Consecrate

Sometimes soe Cleare & soe serene
Itt seemes as't were a looking glass
And to our Vewes presenting seemes
As heauens beneath the waters was
The Sun in it's soe clearely seene
That contemplatinge this bright sight
[p 563] As't was a doubt whether itt had beene
Himselfe or image gaue the light
Att first appearing to our eyes
As if he had falne from the skyes

Thus Meadon whose loue inioynes
To thinke for thee noe labor paine
Receaue these Rustick Shepheards lines
That's from their liuinge objects tane
Sence I seeke only desert places
Wher all alone my thoughts doe use
Noe entertainment but what pleases
The genius of my Rural Muse
But noe thoughts more delighteth mee
Then sweet Remembrances of thee

Que c'est une chose agreable
D'estre sur le bord de la mer,
Quand elle vient a se calmer
Apres quelque orage effroyable!
Et que les chevelus Tritons,
Hauts, sur les vagues secouees,
Frapent les airs d'estranges tons
Avec leurs trompes enrouees,
Dont l'eclat rend respectueux
Les vents les plus impetueux

Tantost l'onde, brouillant l'arene,
Murmure et fremit de courroux,
Se roullant dessus les cailloux
Qu'elle apporte et qu'elle r'entraine
Tantost, elle estale en ses bords,
Que l'ire de Neptune outrage,
Des gens noyez des monstres morts,
Des vaisseaux brisez du naufrage,
Des diamans, de l'ambre gris,
Et mille autres choses de pris

Tantost, la plus claire du monde,
Elle semble un miroir flottant,
Et nous represente a l'instant
Encore d'autres cieux sous l'onde
Le soleil s'y fait si bien voir,
Y comtemplant son beau visage,
Qu'on est quelque temps a sçavoir
Si c'est luy-mesme, ou son image
Et d'abord il semble a nos yeux
Qu'il s'est laisse tomber des cieux

Bernieres pour qui je me vante
De ne rien faire que de beau,
Reçoy ce fantasque tableau
Fait d'une peinture vivante
Je ne cherche que les deserts,
Ou, resvant tout seul, je m'amuse
A des discours assez diserts
De mon genie avec la muse,
Mais mon plus aymable entretien
C'est le ressouvenir du tien[1]

[1] *Fairfax omits the two concluding stanzas*

[p 564] Of a Faire Wife

to Coregio

Thou thinkst Coregio thou hast gott
An excelent Beauty to thy lott
But yet remember this againe
For pleasure also thou'lt haue paine
No perfect rest can be to thee
When watchfull always thou must be
Tis hard & difficult to keepe
That all the world desire & seeke
Is her beauty much, Then know
Her pride's noe less wch she doth show
[p 565] Dost thou admire her the more will shee
For thy esteeme disdainfull be
But is shee faire Consider this
If shee be chast, some doubt it is
As shee in hansomnes exceeds
Soe much of Modesty shee needs
Shee'l alwayes be a Mistress there
Wher only thou Comand should beare
But wouldst thou haue me to define
This rare beauty that is thine
Thy Idoll as thou make's of itt
Much more of Hurt then good thou'le gett
[p 566] For th' Adoration by thee giuen
Giues thee a Hell insteade of Heauen
New habits daly shee will axe
And if denyed then shee will vex
And thinke all's nothing in her passion
That's nott in the Mode & fashion
As if her Body were assign'd
To giue Inquietude's to thy minde
Me thinke I see thee rauisht on her
Thou blinde (as Idolizinge) Louer
Ma'as soone begett Ixion's brood
On Juno's Image in a cloude

[p 567] Why shouldst thou longer thus submit
To her who to obay's more fitt
Least when thy Reason once is lost
Thy Liberty too itt will Cost
And in the end butt as a slaue
A soueraine for Companion haue
To say noe worse of Beauty I Conclude
It is but an Illustrious seruitude

[p 568] Of Beauty

Beauty's a fraile & brittle good
Wch Sicknes Time & Age doe blast
The Rose & Lilly in face thatt budd
Hardly are keept & seldome last
What hath she then to boast on Saue
A fragil life & timely graue

Beauty wher sweet Graces faile
May be Compared vnto this
A goodly ship wth out her saile
A spring her fragrant flower doe miss
[p 569] A day want's Sun or Torch itts Light
A shrine want's Saint or Starless night

But how doth Nature seeme to smother
The Virtues of this louely Flower
Who is of wanton Lust the Mother
Of toyinge Vanity a Bowre
Enmy of Peace the Fount wher Pride doe swime
Th' Incendeary of Strife of Passions Magazen

[p 570] Vpon a Patch Face

Noe Beauty Spots should ladyes weare
They but the Spots of beauty are
Who knowes nott this (saue foolish Sotts)
That Beauty aught to haue noe Spotts
Some note a Spot that Venus had
Admitt itt were in one soe badd
Yett should nott shee haue Spots vpon Her
That would be held a Maide of Honor

[p 571] Vpon an ill Husband

All Creaturs else on Earth that are
Whether they Peace affect or Warre
Males ther Females neuer opress
By the Lyon safe lyes the Lyoness
[p 572] The Beares ther Mates noe harme procure
Wth Wolfe the shee Woolfe liues secure
And of the Bull the Earth wch teeres
The tender Heyfer hts noe feares
But men then these more brutish are
Who wth ther wiues Contend & jarre

[p 572] Of Enuy

In Enuy's Face discerne I this
Of Monsters shee most Monstrous is
A hurtfull glance her eye doth dart
A painfull paine lies att her hart
[p 573] Noe Good does Man enioy by Right
Her enuious teeth doth nott bitte
To Caracterize her yitt more fitt
Of Erringe blindness shee the Pitt
A Hell to Natures swetest Life
Reuenges Spur the flame of Strife
Her Actions yett bespeake her worse
To Ciuill Peace a vexinge Curse
Temptations Sargent thats assignd
The Sentinell of Restless minde
More hurtfull to the soule by farr
Then Vipers to the body are
But in a word texpress this Euell
Tis the Sin peculier to the Diuill

[p 574] Of Anger

Noe Passion's rooted deeper or extends
Her branches further or that more offends
Then Coller doth of wch no sex or Age
Can boast a full exemption from its rage
And when its boundless fury growes
Its high distemper Madnes showes

Soe oft as Man is Angery oh tis sadd
Hes nott only weake but blinde & Madd
Error for Truth imbraces & t wer well
If dearest friends from enmys he Could tell
A harmeless smile or from the eye a glance
Though vndesign d puts him into a trance
[p 575] And when his fury wakes how oft tis seene
Frendships most sacred bonds disolued haue beene
Who doth nott then discerne in sundry fashions
How Man afflicted is wth Angry passions
More fierce then are some Brutes as may apeare
They sometimes yeilds but he s in full Cariere
As Mariners when wth amazement smitt
The Pilots voyce in stormes regards nott itt
Soe men in frenzy ther strange gesters are
Wild as the beasts & Irreguler
The flaminge fire wch Passions kindle flies
In furious sparkes from his pierceinge eyes
His angry face by a reflux of blood
That from his Hart assends becometh rude
[p 576] His haire wth gastly horror stands vpright
And euery word he speakes he seemes to bitt
His hands & feet in ther excentrick Motions
Breath naught but threats wth rash & bloody notions
His Lookes soe terrible as doe portend
A fatal Change vnto his nearest freind
What must be then s distempred soule wthin
Soe vgly outward, but a sinke of Sin

[p 577] Of Virtue

As wel tun d Musick sweetly seize
The sences soe doth't Virtue please
The Virtuous, force the Vitious too
Th'admire in others what they should doe
Those best loue virtue & her lawes
That most Contemnes men's vains aplaues
Vertue alone all Grace inhance
And she noe vse doth make of chance
Whose effects are transcent in th euent
What proceeds from virtue s permenent

Those things itt slights the World doe hold
Pretious as Fortunes Goods & Gold
[p 578] These hath ther wings & flye away
When Man desireth most ther Stay
The virtious Soule prize most that some
Thinkes but from sheepesh nature Come
And nott from Grace the spring frō whence
Flowes Virtue Goodnes Inocence
Care thou for these sence they'le apeare
Much surer Goods then Riches are
Thy virtious acts goe wher thou will
For Companions thou shalt haue still
When Men shall faile & freindship both
A better frende wth thee then goeth
Enuy att death shal Cease in Foes
No Post-hume euel Malice knowes
[p 579] In transendent light shal vertue shine
Wher feet of Enuy Can not clime
Virtue alone doth death outliue
As't twer againe new life doth giue
Whilst Goods of Fortune here haue ends
Virtue alone to heauen assends

[p 582] Nature & Fortune

What thing is nature we may thus define
God draws't through Beings in directst line
Wher as in Fortune soe miscal'd by some
More Crooked is & in Meanders runne
As Natur's rule by prouidence deuine
Soe Fortune too in an obstrucer line
Then Fortune is not blinde as vaine men says
T'is they are blinde discerning not her wayes

[p 583] The Christian War-fare

The marke of note Gods children here doe beare
Is from the Worlds a different Caracter
He to th one for portion here beneath
Doth Losses, Shame & Pouerty bequeath

Yett happy those Afflictions wee account
That to the State Eternal doe amount
The worldly brood if we Caractrize
Th haue noe Afflictions liue in Paridize
Ther Riches here as they desire augment
Ther Honors too increase to ther Content
But as a dreame these Honers vanish soone
And an eternal woe shal take ther Roome
As fatt of Lambes away they shall Consume
Ther Honor vanish into smoke & fume
[p 581] T indure sorrowes & Iniuryes we must
(As Scriptures tel) & be to exile thrust
Then tis a signe indeed heauen is our choyse
When in our Tribulations wee reioyce
T is Gileads pretious Balme & serues to binde
The wounds & blowes wch here below we finde
Yea happy choyse though thus the World vs treat
Seing that in heauen our reward is great
The Soulder of that name vnworthy is
That trembles att the sight of enimyes
Soe is the Christian wch that title bear's
If he att threats of aduerse destine fear s
But wth a patient calmness lett s receaue
What the Soueraigne hand is pleas d to giue
[p 585] The Midle Region or those parts aboue
Are least obscur d nor ther doe Tempests moue
Soe should our soules be rays d boue Passions sphere
Noe Stormes of Tongues Nor Cloudes of enuy feare
In fronts of Batailes we our fortunes Sett
The Ship at Sea wth stormy winds is bett
The Pilot scapt from former gusts noe more
Feare's ship-wrack now then what he did before
The Soulder oft to frequent perills knowne
Neglects the danger that s soe Comon growne
And soe should we when our Afflictions growe
Wth lenghtned Patience learne to beare them too
This Life s a war-fare if sometimes begun
To parly wth our sorrowes t is soone done
And in th end when hopes begin to Cease
[p 586] Proues but a Cessation noe Continu d Peace
Whilst through cleare skyes the Sun triumphant rides
Vpon a sudden cloudes his splendor hides

Doth health & Pleasure spur our sences on
Soon sickness Comes and all delights are gone
Such is the State of vs vncertaine men
To know in calmes to guide our Vessels then
Is not enough, but t'is when Tempests rise
To steare a Course both Patient, Stout, & Wise
Did our misfortunes soe deuide our share
As some shee would Afflict & others Spare
We might Complaine of her inconstant fitts
Bullets as soon th Captaine as soulder hitts
The Feauer to the Great a deafe eare hath
[p 587] As to the meanest both subuerts by death
Soe may the Justice of Impartial fate
For Comfort serue vs in our greatest Strait
Why doe we enuy then aspiringe Men
Wth Stormes the Vallyes are less troubled then
The lofty Hills & humble shrubbs belowe
Less dangers in then Oakes that highest growe[1]
See we not how the straitest Popler tree
And spredinge Elme as they vngratfull be
For nurishment) to barreness incline
Whilst prostrate on the ground the Crocked vine
Abundance yeilds or haue we nott seene
From highest plenty men in wants haue beene
How many Kings falne from their Regall seate
Haue Crackt their Crownes their Royal Septers breake
[p 588] Our Wittnesses by cloudes we all may bringe
To shew that splendid honours a vaine thinge
Should they be tane from vs resolue thus much
Their loss should not be great their fadinges such
Should we afflict ourselues when loss appears
Our Teares would sooner want then Cause for teares
All you wth heauenly Marks of God indued
Arme to the Fight shew Virtue Fortitude
As Rocks 'gainst wch the raging billowes rore
Keepe firme their station on the threatned shore
Soe let our Soules be firme & Constant still
Against the threats this World doth make of Ill
Or as a Diamon mongst the dust doth dart
The beauty more in its resplendent sparke

[1] Cf Horace, *Carm* II 10

[p 589] In midst of troubles soe lett vs demeane
As Countinances be pleasant Soules serene
Remember t'is from high Aflictions fall
From Prouidence deuine that gouern's all
Who when he please in turning of an eye
Turns Wrath to Mercy Sorrows into Joy
T'is he who made the fertile Earth produce
Her annual fruit most meet for humane vse
He both the Rose & Violets did Cloth
T'is he beauty & th'oders gaue to both
Twas his Almighty power that did make fall
Att Israels seige the Jerecoman Wall
That ons Enmyes ruing he might raise
Trophy on Trophy to inrich his Prayse
[p. 590] Shal we then those his wonders now less prize
Or thinke his Power abat's, or hee less wise
No, hee's as able still Nor shall His want
Victory on Standards Glory on ther front

[p 590] Life & Death Compared together

Such vulgar thoughts the World doe fill
To thinke Life good Death only ill
Then life ill liued noe euell's worse
Death (dieing well) remoues the Curse
And t'is for certaine truth men tell
He ne're dies ill that liueth well
Ill liues doe but ther Ills increase
[p 591] But dieng well makes Euells Cease
Badd men haite death but not soe much
That itt is Ill, as They are such
Moral Men teache vs in their bookes
That we should despise death's grime lookes
T'is Comõn sence wch doth inspire
Ther feares of thatt Good men desire
Nor Can we truly death define
By makinge odious what's sublime
Consider t in th' effects & soe itt will
Plead much for death be't Good or Ill
Say itt be Ill yett here's the Good
To greater Ills it giues a period
In life what one good thinge is ther

[p 592] To keepe our Passions Reguler
The many Ills each day is done
Makes Death less fear'd but once to come
But rather thanke Death thats the Cause
Our Ills are not Imortal Lawes

[p 592] Vpon a Fontaine

Seest thou how these waters flowe
How soone againe away itt glides
Soe worldly Glory's but a showe
That neuer long wth vs abides[1]

[p 593] Vpon the New-built
House att Apleton

Thinke not ô Man that dwells herein
This House's a Stay but as an Inne
Wch for Conuenience fittly stands
In way to one nott made wth hands
But if a time here thou take Rest
Yett thinke Eternity's the Best

[p 594] Shortness of Life

In Rosy morne I saw Aurora red
But when the Sun his beames had fully spred
She vanisht I saw a Frost then a Dew
T'wixt time soe short as scarce a time I knew
This stranger seemd when in more raised thought
I saw Death Come How soone a life he'ad Caught
Wher in the turninge of an eye he ad done
Farre Speedier execution then the Sun

---

[1] Pour une Fontaine
Vois tu, passant, couler cette onde
Et s'écouler incontinent ?
Ainsi fuit la gloire du monde
Et rien que Dieu n'est permanent Malherbe

[p 595] Epitaph on A V dieng Younge

O what affront was itt to Nature
And sadder Influence of the Skyes
That in a moment closd the Eyes
Of such a machless Creature
But askinge what might be the Reason
That Creuel Fate soe out of season
Had Caried her from vs soe farre
This Answer was to me returnd
Least that the Earth should bee burnd
By th scorching beames of that bright starr

[p 596] The Lady Caryes
Elogy on my deare Wife

O Fatal fall might not those heapes suffice
This Sumer Captiu'd but thou must surprize
The best of Nobels this soe great good Lady
A Vere A Fairfax Honours-Honour, Shee
Did grace her Birth Sex Relate & Degree
& Shee a Non-parell for Piety
Vers t in the Theory of Godliness
The wch she did in Conference express
Its Practick part her life to life did shew
Each way but most excellinge in all vew
Was Faith Submission vnweared pleasantnes
[p 597] With vniuersal weaknes, Paine Sickness
Many longe lasting Great few euer sence
Soe followed Job in suffringe Patience
But she is now most gloriously exalted
Wher sin & sorrow neuer entred
To Mount Zion heauenly Jerusalem
The City of God to Spirits of Just men
To Church of the first borne to Angels blest
To God to Jesus this Compleats the rest
Her Faith saw this wch made her smile att death
And wth much Joy surrendred vp her breath
Her Body deare her All thats out of Heauen
To Billbrough church as a riche Treasure's giuen
Bilbrough church-yeard dame me a little roome
That after death my graue waite on her Tombe

[p 598] To the Lady Cary

Vpon her Verses on my deare Wife

Madam

Could I a Tribute of my thanks express
As you haue done in loue & purer Verse
On my best selfe then I might Justly raise
Your Elogy t Encomiums of your Prayse
And soe forgett the Subiect that did moue
Me to a thankfulnes as t did you to loue
O t'were to great a Crime but pray allow
Wher I fall short but you haue reached to
Makinge that Good wisest of Kings hath said
Th Liuings not soe Preyse-worthy then the dead
I thinke the Reason's this itts grounded on
Cause Mercys are not priz'd till they are gone
[p 599] O had not hopes surpast my grosser sence
My loss Could not haue had a recompence
Yett such an Influence hath your happy straine
To bring my buried Joy to life againe
Vertue Goodnes Loue things Iṁortalize
The better part when as the other dies
True, Soules in Bodyes haue their being here
But Loues in Soules haue ther ther proper Sphere
Then is true loue Compos'd of Nobler fyers
Then to extinguish when the Life expires
Butt to Conclude Madam me think you spire
In humblest Thoughts to raise your Trophys higher
Then Her's you would attend in gelid Mould
Wch for her Friend the lodging seemes too Could
[p 600] But were itt soe itt my good happ might bee
To lye next Her, To you our Quire is free

[p 600] On the Fatal day

Jan 30 1648

Oh lett that Day from time be blotted quitt
And lett beleefe of't in next Age be waued
In deepest silence th Act Concealed might
Soe that the King-doms Credit might be saued

But if the Power deuine permited this
His Will's the Law & ours must acquiesse

Curæ loquuntur leues
Ingentes stupent

[p 601] Of Inpartial Fate

Here we all the Same Danger run
By the like Destin's we are ledd
Same Misfortune to the Shepeard Come
May attack as well the Crowned head
Our dayes are Spun vpon that wheele
The meanest Subiect & greatest Kinge
To like end th' Fatal Sisters bringe
The thread when Cutt both same Sisers feele

[f 604] A Carracter of the Romish
Church by Francisco Petrarca
Laura Can · 106

Fiamma dal ciel su tue treccie pioua

Heauens dire flame sits on thy Curled tresses
O wrech, from scrip & wallet who's become
Both riche & great through those wch thou oppresses
Soe much reioyces thou when euells Come
A nest of Treasons wher mischeifes bredd
Ther hacht in the o're the World is spred

Wine Bed good Belly chere & pleasant dayes
To All, thy whoredoms to the vttmost shews
[p 605] Thy seruants younge & old the wanton playes
This fire wth bellowes Bel-ze-bub blowes
Such is thy life thou wicked Epicure
As to the Heauens thy stinch is gone vp sure

Fountaine of Greefe & woe wraths harbor too
Temple of Heresy Pitt of Errors deepe
In elter times we held thee Rome but now
Babel the peruerse for wch wee weepe
A shopp of Cousnage prison of Crueltyes
Wher ills mentaind & wher Goodnes dyes

When founded first wast humble Poore & Chast
Thy hornes against thy Founders now thou lifts
[p 606] O shameles Strumpet wher's thy trust now plast
Is't in th' Adultryes ill gott Goods or Shifts
Then vnto All great wonder itt will bee
If Christ in th' End powre nott his wrath on thee[1]

[Fiamma dal ciel su le tue treccie piova,
Malvagia, che dal fiume e dalle ghiande,
Per l'altrui impoverir se' ricca e grande,
Poiche di mal oprar tanto ti giova
Nido di tradimenti in cui si cova
Quanto mal per lo mondo oggi si spande,
Di vin serva, di letti e di vivande,
In cui lussuria fa l'ultima prova
Per le camere tue fanciulle e vecchi
Vanno trescando, e Belzebub in mezzo
Co' mantici e col foco e con gli specchi
Gia non fostu nudrita in piume al rezzo,
Ma nuda al vento, e scalza fra li stecchi
Or vivi si, ch'a Dio ne venga il lezzo

Fontana di dolore, albergo d'ira,
Scola d'errori e tempio d'eresia,
Gia Roma or Babilonia falsa e ria
Per cui tanto si piagne e si sospira
O fucina d'inganni, o prigion dira,
Ove 'l ben more, e 'l mal si nutre e cria.
Di vivi Inferno, un gran miracol fia
Se Cristo teco alfine non s'adira
Fondata in casta ed umil povertate,
Contra tuoi fondatori alzi le corna.
Putta sfacciata e dov' hai posto spene?
Negli adulterj tuoi, nelle malnate
Ricchezze tante? Or Constantin non torna
Ma tolga il mondo triste che 'l sostene[2]]

[1] See page 215
[2] These sonnets are not in the MS

[p 612] Vpon the Horse wch his Matie
Rode vpon att his Coronation 1660

Hence then Dispaire my hopes why should itt bury
Sence this braue Steed Bredd first was in my Query
Now thus aduanct wth highest honors loden
Whilst his that bredd him on by most Mens troden
But t is noe matter Seing tho' hast gott th' Aduance
Then please the Royal Rider wth thy Prance
Soe may thy Fame much rayse thy Prayses higher
Then Chessnut that begott the or Brid-la-dore his Sire

Bridla dore (Anglice)
Golden Bridle

[p 613] Vulgar Proverbs

None to another frend can be
That to himselfe's an enmy

[p 614] Of sence & Money & of Faith
Where's the Man that too much hath

Betwixt the Bridle & the Spur
Reason often lodgeth her

In th' house of Foes prepose this End
To gett some Woman for thy frend

[p 615] The Hope of Game—Abateth paine

Wouldst thou have all thy troubles cease
Then see & heare & hold thy peace

Lait (doe we say) repents the Ratt
When by the Neck has hold the Catt

His thoughts are good & ever best
That carryes Death wthin his brest

[p 617] A fatt Earth makes a Horse to labour
But A good Lawyer is an ill Neighbour

Make Night of Night & Day of Day
Soe wth less sorrow live you may

[p 618] Pardon to Men that evel be
Unto the God's an injury

When Pride on horseback getteth upp
Loss & shame sitts on the Croup

[p 620] He that would live in healthfulnes
Must dine wth little & supp wth less

[p 621] As the evening doth the day comend
So life is Praysed by the end

[p 622] Virtue shewes the greater grace
Shining from a bautious face

[p 624] Att a rounde Table noe Strife is
Who shal be nearest a good Dish

Dry March Wett April May thats both
Brings plenty wher ther is noe sloth

[p 625] In a fresh gale
Extend thy Saile

[p 626] We may be sure still innocence
Beares in itselfe its owne defence

[p 627] To read & yitt to have learnd nought
Is like the chase wher nothing's caught

[p 628] Tis good we should the tongue comand
Speake litle & more understand
For if from us our words once fall
It is too late them to recall

Humane Praise Is a vaine blaze

[p 631] Sett on a Seat a Foole ere longe
Hele wagg his Legges or sing a songe

[p 633] Nature made nothing so sublime
Butt Virtue to the topp will clime

When a whit frost on earth doth lie
Tis a presage then raine is nie

[p 635] On a womans first Counsel rest
Seldome the Second is the best

Bread Butter & good Cheese
A shield gainst death be al these

Pardon give to every one
But to thyselfe alow none

[p. 637] When Italy is without Fish
When France without Treason is
In England longe noe war we see
Then without Earth the World shall bee

[p. 638] My contry is in all lands wher
I goe & meet with true friends ther

[p 641] The teares of France for the deplorable death of Henry 4 surnamed the Great

Ah is itt then Great Henry soe fam'd
For taming men himselfe by death is tam'd
Whatt eye his glory saw now his sad doome
But must desolue in Teares sigh out his Soule
Soe small a shred of Earth should him intombe
Whos acts deseru'd pocession of the whole

O tis but fitt for joyes we henceforth mourne
Our songes & mirth into sad plaints we turne
Instead of this great King greefe may raigne here
So thatt in sorrow plung'd our fainting breath
May send our endless sighs to th'highst Sphere
Whilst hopless teares distill vpon the earth

[p 642] Yes itt is fitt what else can we returne
Butt teares as offrings to his sacred vrne
Wth them his Sable Marble tombe bedew
No no such armes too weake sence itt apeares
For vs he of his blood too careless grew
Haue we naught else for him butt a few teares

O could our eyes to fontains we distill
T' Would nott abate the least part of our ill
We oft shed teares for simple wrongs oft weepe
Too Coñon oft for things of lesser prise
Then lett vs die att this great Monarchs feet
His Tombe th' Alter our selues the sacrifice

But who can die if Sisters Fate denies
A closure to our full death trickling eyes
Hauing shut vp those of this warlike Prince
Atropos so proud is of her royal pray
Her Cypriss into Laurels will turne Sence
Of this great Victor she hath gott the day

[p 643] But sence we are ordain'd to sigh & liue
And after this their fatall stroke then giue
Liue then complaining this sad shock of Fate
When happy days are gone no joy appeares
Then mourne & sigh till death our greefe abate
And shew whilst liuing, Life shal wast in teares

[1] Quoi ? faut-il que Henri, ce redouté monarque,
Ce dompteur des humains, soit dompté par la Parque ?
Que l'œil qui vit sa gloire ores voye sa fin ?
Que le nostre pour lui incessamment degoutte ?
Et que si peu de terre enferme dans son sein
Celui qui meritoit de la posseder toute ?

Quoi ? faut-il qu'à jamais nos joies soyent esteintes ?
Que nos chants et nos ris soyent convertis en plaintes ?
Qu'au lieu de nostre roi le deuil regne en ces lieux ?
Que la douleur nous poigne et le regret nous serre ?
Que sans fin nos souspirs montent dedans les cieux ?
Que sans espoir nos pleurs descendent sur la terre ?

Il le faut, on le doit. Et que pouvons-nous rendre
Que des pleurs assidus à cette auguste cendre ?
Arrousons à jamais son marbre triste blanc.
Non, non, plustost quittons ces inutiles armes !
Mais puisqu'il fut pour nous prodigue de son sang,
Serions-nous bien pour lui avares de nos larmes ?

Quand bien nos yeux seroyent convertis en fontaines,
Ils ne sauroyent noyer la moindre de nos peines.
On espanche des pleurs pour un simple meschef,
Un devoir trop commun bien souvent peu s'estime.
Il faut doncques mourir aux pieds de nostre chef.
Son tombeau soit l'autel et nos corps la victime.

Mais qui pourroit mourir ? Les Parques filandieres
Desdaignent de toucher à nos mortes paupieres,
Ayans fermé les yeux du prince des guerriers.
Atropos de sa proye est par trop glorieuse.
Elle peut bien changer ses cypres en lauriers,
Puisque de ce vainqueur elle est victorieuse.

Puisqu'il nous faut encor et souspirer et vivre,
Puisque la Parque fuit ceux qui la veulent suivre,
Vivons donc en plaignant nostre rigoureux sort,
Nostre bonheur perdu, nostre joye ravie,
Lamentons, souspirons, et jusques à la mort
Tesmoignons qu'en vivant nous pleurons nostre vie.

[1] See page 246. This is not in the MS.

Bewaile bewaile this our great Monarchs fall
Of Judgment perfait humour pleasing all
His equal none a Hart wthout all feare
Perfection such t'would but fall short in prayse
Enough to haue serued a World to' haue admird here
Had nott his equal Justice bound his wayes

Lament lament this Sage & Prudent King
Thatt hight of Bonty vigelence in him
Thatt hart wch could be mou'd not ouercome
Virtues here rarely found though we inquire
Parts I could sooner much admire then sume
Sence this Achilis a Homer would require

[p 644] We cañott count the Splendours of his Glorys
Nor number yitt his signal victorys
O no for such a subiect were too great
We aught to prayse what yitt we cannot write
And hold our peace or to good purpose speake
He nothing saith doth not to th' full recite

His famous acts once raisd our drouping heads
His Laurels from the temples was our shades
End of his Combats ended feares wee're in
Him only prisd dispisd all other Powers
More glorying to be subiect to this King
Then if we'ad had some other Kings for ours

But now this Glory's clouded wth a staine
And now our joy & Mirth ther leaue hath taine
The Lillys fade as we att this sad Fate
Downe to the growne ther drouping heads doe bowe
Seeming as humble as Compassionate
To crowne his Tombe or else him homage doe

[pp 645 646 *are blank*]

Plaignons, pleurons sans fin cet esprit admirable,
Ce jugement parfait, cet' humeur agréable,
Cet hercule sans pair aussi bien que sans peur,
Tant de perfections qu'en loüant on souspire.
Qui pouvoyent asservir le monde à sa valeur,
Si sa rare équité n'eust borné son Empire.

Regrettons, souspirons cette sage prudence,
Cette extrême bonté, cette rare vaillance,
Ce cœur qui se pouvoit fleschir et non dompter.
Vertus de qui la perte est à nous tant amère
Et que je puis plustost admirer que chanter,
Puisqu' à ce grand Achille il faudroit un Homère.

. . . . [1]

Pourroit-on bien conter le nombre de ses gloires?
Pourroit-on bien nombrer ses insignes victoires?
Non, d'un si grand discours le dessein est trop haut.
On doit louër sans fin ce qu'on ne peut escrire,
Il faut humble se taire ou parler comme il faut,
Et celui ne dit rien qui ne peut assez dire.

. . . . [1]

Jadis pour ses beaux faits nous eslevions nos testes,
L'ombre de ses lauriers nous gardoit des tempestes,
La fin de ses combats finissoit nostre effroi.
Nous nous prisions tous seuls, nous mesprisions les autres,
Estant plus glorieux d'estre subjects du roi
Que si les autres rois eussent esté les nostres.

Maintenant nostre gloire est à jamais ternie,
Maintenant nostre joye est pour jamais finie;
Les lys sont atterez et nous avecques eux.
Dafné baisse, chétifve, en terre son visage,
Et semble par ce geste, humble autant que piteux,
Ou couronner sa tombe ou bien lui faire hommage.|

[1] Fairfax omits a stanza here.

AA 000 264 112 4

Lightning Source UK Ltd.
Milton Keynes UK
UKHW020255050319
338417UK00015B/376/P